LIGHTNING BOLT BOOKS™

Red Everywhere

Kristin Sterling

Lerner Publications Company
Minneapolis

Dedicated to people who love red

Lerner Publications Company
A division of Lerner Publishing Group, Inc.
241 First Avenue North
Minneapolis, MN 55401 U.S.A.

Website address: www.lernerbooks.com

Library of Congress Cataloging-in-Publication Data

Sterling, Kristin.
    Red Everywhere / by Kristin Sterling.
       p.   cm. — (Lightning bolt books™—Colors everywhere)
    Includes index.
    ISBN 978-0-7613-4590-9 (lib. bdg. : alk. paper)
    1. Red—Juvenile literature. 2. Colors—Juvenile literature. I. Title.
  QC495.5.S746 2010
  535.6—dc22   2009017955

Manufactured in the United States of America
1 — BP — 12/15/09

Contents

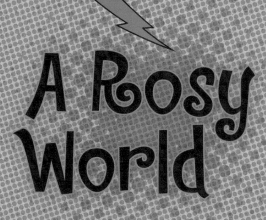

A Rosy World

Do you like warm, exciting colors? Many people love the color red.

Red things can be found in the world around you.

The tulips in this field are red.

A rose makes a beautiful gift for someone you love. Roses are often dark red.

6

Look at this fancy necklace.

It is made out of red gemstones called rubies.

This necklace
has red rubies and
white diamonds.

Where can you find a juicy red snack?

Pick an apple from a tree at an orchard.

You can grow red tomatoes in a garden. Ripe tomatoes make a salad tasty and colorful.

This bright red bird is a cardinal. Only the males are red. Females are brown!

Male and female cardinals sit on a snowy tree branch. Can you tell which is which?

Red strawberries are delicious.
You can eat them on ice
cream sundaes.

People also make things that are red. Fire trucks are painted red.

Fire trucks are red so that they are easy to see.

Women wear red lipstick.
Red clothes make people
stand out in a crowd.

13

Shades of Red

There are many different shades of red. Look for shades of red around your home.

Crimson is a dark red shade. It has a bit of purple in it. Emily's backpack is crimson.

Maroon is a deep, dark red. Actors take a bow in front of a maroon curtain onstage.

Most stage curtains are a shade of red.

Scarlet is a bright red color. Jessie is wearing a scarlet sweater.

Blush is a light, pinkish shade of red. This juice is blush colored.

Seeing Red

Are you seeing red?

Or do you see the world through rose-colored glasses?

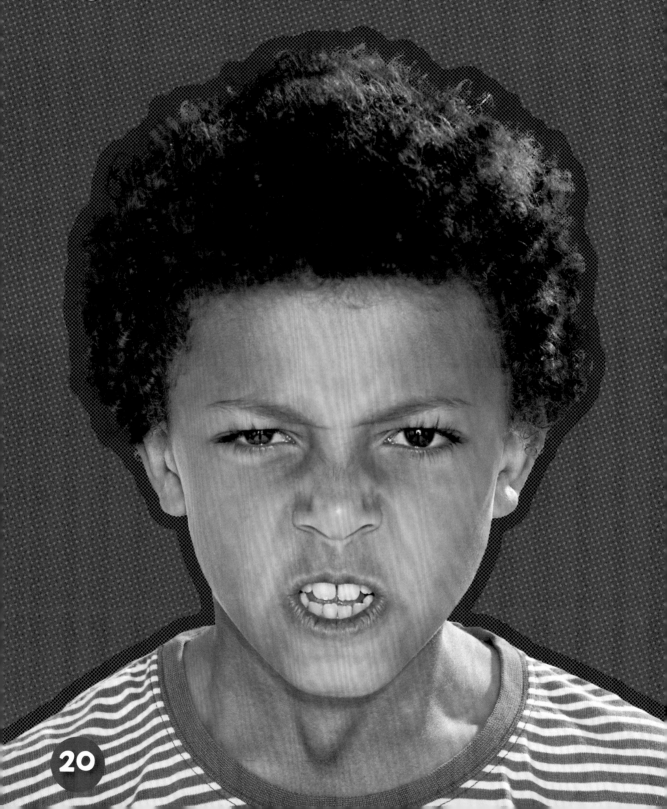

"Seeing red" means that you are angry or annoyed.

20

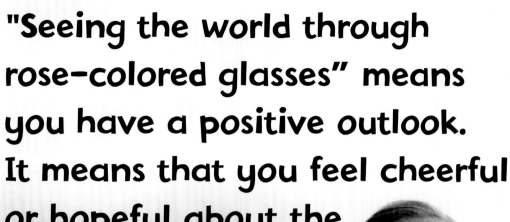

"Seeing the world through rose-colored glasses" means you have a positive outlook. It means that you feel cheerful or hopeful about the way things are.

Lizzy thinks this is a perfect day for a picnic—even though it looks as if it might rain.

21

Do you think red is an angry or hopeful color?

This family is wearing different shades of red. How many shades do you see?

22

Ricky and Robert Love Red

Ricky and Robert think red is an exciting color. They love it!

They wear red clothes all the time. They even have red hair!

Their mom drives a red car. They live in a red apartment building.

Pepleri 6

25

Ricky likes to eat red snow cones at the fair.

Snow cones are a sweet, cool treat on a hot summer day.

What is your favorite color?

Fun Facts

- Red is a very strong color. It is easy to see. Stop signs and brake lights are red because the color makes people pay attention.

- About two in one hundred people in the world have red hair.

- Red is a lucky color in China. Women wear red dresses when they get married.

seeing the color red makes your heart beat faster.

Tomato frogs are a bright red color. The color is a warning to other animals to stay away!

Bullfighters wave a red cape in front of a bull to make it angry. The color is not what makes the bull angry. Bulls are color-blind! The movement of the cape makes the bull angry.

Mars is called the Red Planet because its surface is reddish

Glossary

annoyed: to be disturbed or irritated

gemstone: a stone that can be cut and used in jewelry

orchard: a place where fruit or nut trees are grown

outlook: point of view

positive: hopeful or good

ripe: ready to be eaten

Further Reading

Enchanted Learning: Red
http://www.enchantedlearning.com/colors/red.shtml

Hamanaka, Sheila. *All the Colors of the Earth.*
New York: Morrow Junior Books, 1994.

Jenkins, Steve. *Living Color.* Boston: Houghton
Mifflin, 2007.

Learn about Color!
http://www.metmuseum.org/explore/Learn_About_
Color/index.html

Lionni, Leo. *A Color of His Own.* New York: A. A.
Knopf, 2006.

Ross, Kathy. *Kathy Ross Crafts Colors.*
Minneapolis: Millbrook Press, 2003.

Index

Photo Acknowledgments

The images in this book are used with the permission of: © age fotostock/SuperStock, pp. 1, 29; © Robert Manella/Stone/Getty Images, p. 2; © iStockphoto.com/Ben Blankenburg, p. 4; © Katarzyna Mazurowska/Dreamstime.com, p. 5; © George Doyle/ Stockbyte/Getty Images, p. 6; © SuperStock/SuperStock, p. 7; © Juliette Wade/Garden Picture Library/Photolibrary, p. 8; © Blend Images/Photoshot , p. 9; © iStockphoto.com/ Tony Campbell, p. 10; © Tom Grill/Iconica/Getty Images, p. 11; © Digitalphotonut/ Dreamstime.com, p. 12; © Ryan McVay/Stone+/Getty Images, p. 13; © iStockphoto.com/ Ilya Lugvinev, p. 14; © Ryan McVay/Photodisc/Getty Images, p. 15; © John Giustina/ Iconica/Getty Images, p. 16; © Lucas Allen/Lifesize/Getty Images, p. 17; © Eaglemoss Consumer Publications/Fresh Food Images/Photolibrary, p. 18; © Ryan McVay/Lifesize/ Getty Images, p. 19; © Tom Merton/OJO Images/Getty Images, p. 20; © Soren Hald/Digital Vision/Getty Images, p. 21; © Alex Mares-Manton/Asia Images/Getty Images, p. 22; © iStockphoto.com/Pete Collins, pp. 23, 24; © Focus Database/Tips Italia/Photolibrary, p. 25; © Kathryn Russell Studios/FoodPix/Getty Images, p. 26; © Hans Neleman/The Image Bank/Getty Images, p. 27; © Altrendo images/Getty Images, p. 28; © Jose Manuel Gelpi Diaz/Dreamstime.com, p. 30; © Baerbel Schmidt/Taxi/Getty Images, p. 31.

Cover: © Alxpin/Dreamstime.com (tomato); © Anthony Aneese Totah Jr/Dreamstime. com (fire truck); © Justin Maresch/Dreamstime.com (paint brush); © Rusty Dodson/ Dreamstime.com (bird); © Olga Lyubkina/Dreamstime.com (apple); © Todd Strand/ Independent Picture Service (paint strips).